ASIAN
COUNTRIES
TODAY

CHINA

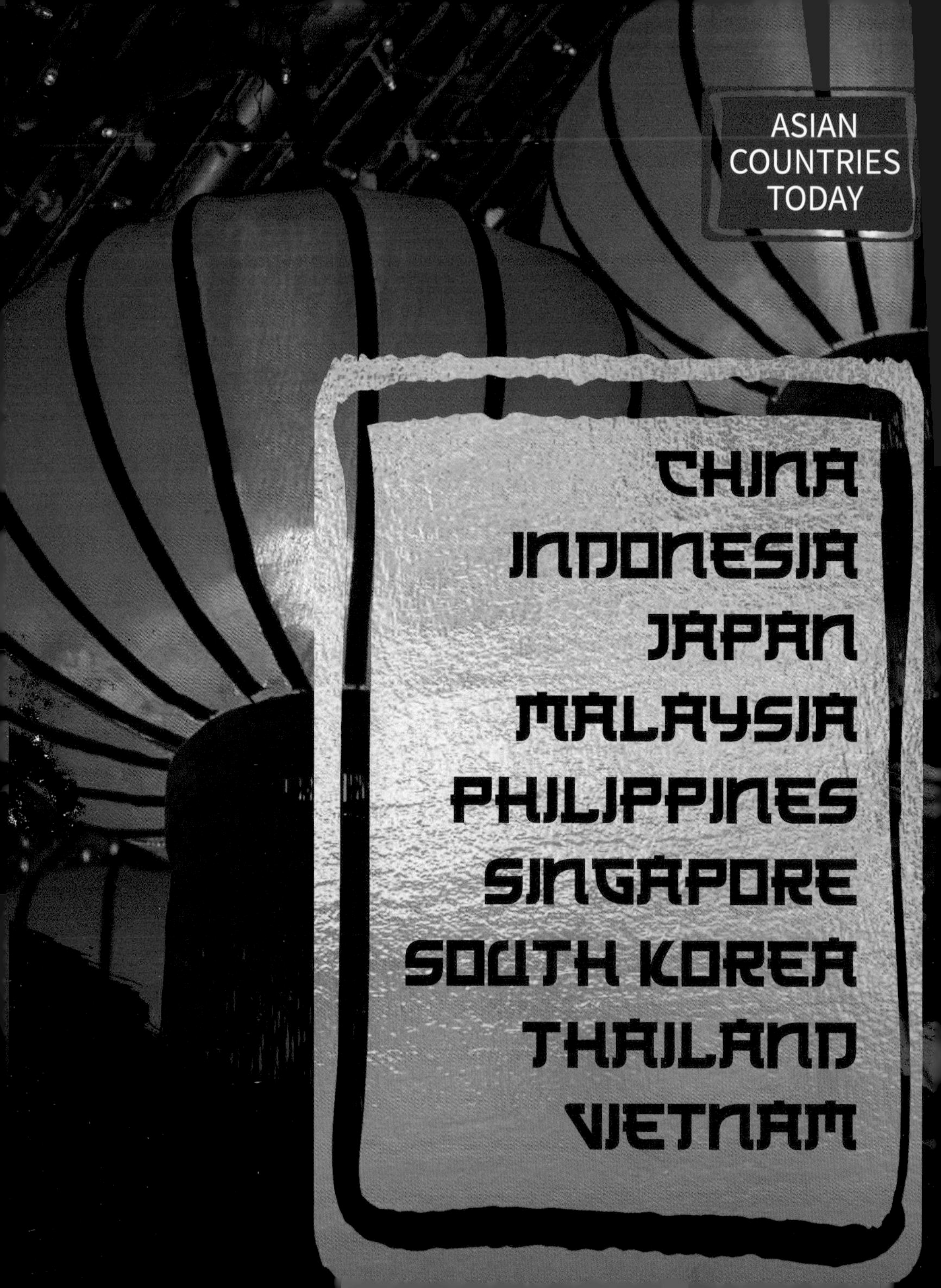

ASIAN COUNTRIES TODAY

CHINA
INDONESIA
JAPAN
MALAYSIA
PHILIPPINES
SINGAPORE
SOUTH KOREA
THAILAND
VIETNAM

ASIAN
COUNTRIES
TODAY

CHINA

JENNIFER BROWN

MASON CREST
PHILADELPHIA
MIAMI

MASON CREST

450 Parkway Drive, Suite D, Broomall, Pennsylvania 19008
(866) MCP-BOOK (toll-free) • www.masoncrest.com

Printed in the United States of America

First printing
9 8 7 6 5 4 3 2 1

ISBN (hardback) 978-1-4222-4264-3
ISBN (series) 978-1-4222-4263-6
ISBN (ebook) 978-1-4222-7550-4

Cataloging-in-Publication Data on file with the Library of Congress

Developed and Produced by National Highlights Inc.
Editor: Susan Uttendorfsky
Interior and cover design: Jana Rade
Production: Michelle Luke

NATIONAL
HIGHLIGHTS

CONTENTS

KEY ICONS TO LOOK FOR:

 WORDS TO UNDERSTAND: These words with their easy-to-understand definitions will increase the reader's understanding of the text while building vocabulary skills.

 SIDEBARS: This boxed material within the main text allows readers to build knowledge, gain insights, explore possibilities, and broaden their perspectives by weaving together additional information to provide realistic and holistic perspectives.

 EDUCATIONAL VIDEOS: Readers can view videos by scanning our QR codes, providing them with additional educational content to supplement the text. Examples include news coverage, moments in history, speeches, iconic sports moments, and much more!

 TEXT-DEPENDENT QUESTIONS: These questions send the reader back to the text for more careful attention to the evidence presented there.

 RESEARCH PROJECTS: Readers are pointed toward areas of further inquiry connected to each chapter. Suggestions are provided for projects that encourage deeper research and analysis.

 SERIES GLOSSARY OF KEY TERMS: This back-of-the-book glossary contains terminology used throughout this series. Words found here increase the reader's ability to read and comprehend higher-level books and articles in this field.

CHINA AT A GLANCE

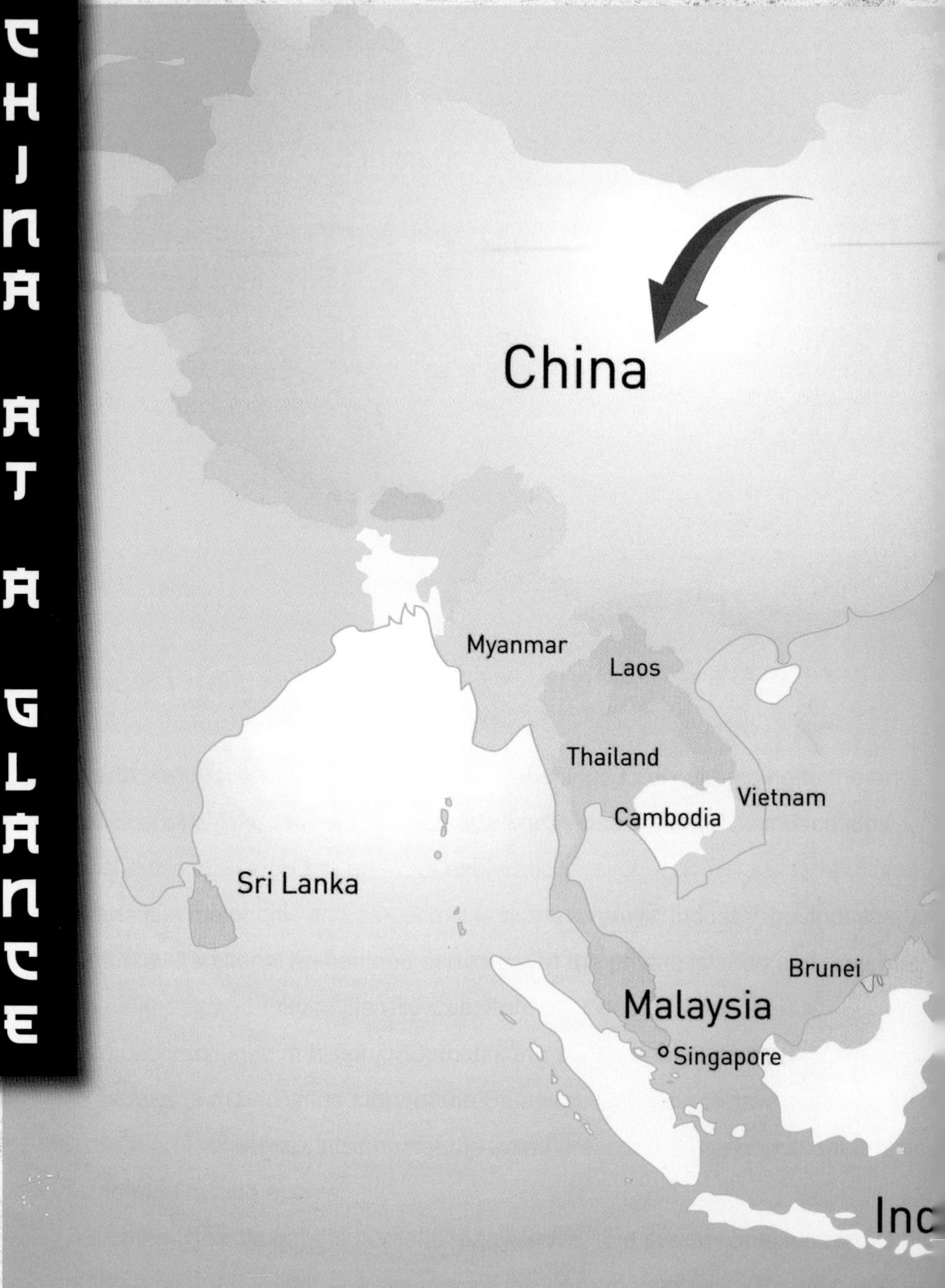
China
Myanmar
Laos
Thailand
Cambodia
Vietnam
Sri Lanka
Brunei
Malaysia
Singapore
Inc

North Korea

South Korea

Japan

hilippines

The Geography of China

Location:
China is located in Eastern Asia, bordering the South China Sea, Yellow Sea, Korea Bay, and East China Sea between Vietnam and North Korea

Area: Slightly larger than the United States of America
total: 3,705,406 sq. miles (9,956,960 sq. km)
land: 3,600,947 sq. miles (9,326,410 sq. km)
water: 104,459 sq. miles (270,550 sq. km)

Borders: China shares its border with fourteen countries, which include: Afghanistan, Bhutan, Burma, India, Kazakhstan, North Korea, Kyrgyzstan, Laos, Mongolia, Nepal, Pakistan, Russia, Tajikistan, and Vietnam

Climate: Ranges from extremely hot summers to extremely cold winters

Terrain: A diverse landscape, from flat plains, mountains, and lowlands

Elevation Extremes:
lowest point: Turpan Pendi, at 505 feet (154 meters) below sea level

highest point: Mount Everest, at 29,028 feet (8,848 meters)

Natural Hazards:
earthquakes, flooding, and drought

Source: www.cia.gov 2017

Originally adopted on October 1, 1949, the Chinese flag is red in color, which symbolizes the Chinese Communist Revolution. Red is also considered the traditional color of the Chinese people. The largest gold star on the flag stands for communism and the four smaller stars are there to represent each of the social classes of the Chinese people. Also, the five stars altogether show the importance that has been placed on the number five within Chinese history and philosophy.

The People of China

Population: 1,384,688,986

Ethnic Groups: Han Chinese Zhuang, other (includes Hui, Manchu, Uighur, Miao, Yi, Tujia, Tibetan, Mongol, Dong, Buyei, Yao, Bai, Korean, Hani, Li, Kazakh, Dai

Age Structure:
> 0–14 years: 17.22% (238,390,960)
> 15–24 years: 12.32% (170,634,865)
> 25–54 years: 47.84% (662,369,118)
> 55–64 years: 11.35% (157,198,197)
> 65 years and over: 11.27% (156,105,900)

Population Growth Rate:
> 0.37%

Death Rate:
> 8 deaths/1,000 pop.

Migration Rate:
> -0.4 migrant(s)/1,000 pop.

Infant Mortality Rate:
> 11.8 deaths/1,000 live births

Life Expectancy at Birth:
> total population: 75.8 years
> male: 73.7 years
> female: 78.1 years

Total Fertility Rate:
> 1.6 children born/woman

Religions:
> Buddhist, Christian, Muslim, Folk, Hindu, Jewish, Taoist

Languages:
> Standard Chinese or Mandarin is the official language, other dialects, Mongolian, Tibetan

Literacy Rate:
> 96.4%

Source: www.cia.gov 2018

The Li River with the Karst mountains in the background, Guangxi Province.

foothills: hills at the bottom of higher hills

populous: having a large, dense population in a limited amount of space; the whole number of people in a country or region

topography: the features (such as mountains and rivers) in an area of land

CHINA'S GEOGRAPHY & LANDSCAPE

CHAPTER 1

Geography

Welcome to China! Of all the Asian countries, China is the world's most **populous** nation. Also, China has a rich history that spans more than 4,000 years. Many of the elements that make up the foundation of the modern world actually originated in China. This includes things such as paper money, the compass, credit banking, gunpowder, and paper. Now the country has the fastest growing economy in the world and is currently in a period that many refer to as the Second Industrial Revolution.

China is one of the world's top exporters and has a diverse terrain where you can find large plateaus, mountains, and more.

The large, crowded country is one that many people strive to understand. Learn more about Chinese geography, climate, and flora and fauna by reading the information found here. Doing so provides insight into the layout and environment that people live in this country.

China is located in Southeast Asia on the coastline of the Pacific Ocean. It is the third largest country in the world, coming in behind Russia and Canada. Taking up a total area of 3.7 million square miles (9.6 million square kilometers), with a coastline of 11,184 miles (18,000 kilometers), the shape of China when you look on a map is similar to that of a rooster. On the northern end, China reaches up to the Heliongjang province, and Zengmu Ansha is found to the far south. On the west is Pamirs, with the eastern border being found along the Wusuli River and Heilongjiang River.

Fourteen different countries make up the border of China, including Afghanistan, Bhutan, Burma, India, Kazakhstan, North Korea, Kyrgyzstan, Laos, Mongolia, Nepal, Pakistan, Russia, Tajikstan, and Vietnam.

When it comes to physical features of the country, a diverse grouping exists, consisting of mountains, **foothills**, basins, plains, and plateaus. Nearly two-thirds of the land is made up of rugged mountains, foothills, and plateaus. The land is higher in the west than in the east—similar in construction to a three-step ladder.

The Cloud Sea at Mount Huang

This location is considered one of the top four unique natural wonders found on Mount Huang. Since ancient times, the Yellow Mountain has also been called the Yellow Sea—a shadowy fairyland where the steep peaks are hidden behind mist and thick clouds. The mist on Mount Huang, an amazing phenomenon, occurs over 200 days of the year, and the Cloud Sea can be seen most of the year. This mountain area offers an amazing experience for those who visit and is something that everyone should see!

The top step of this "ladder **topography**" is created by what is known as the Qinghai-Tibet Plateau, which has an average height of more than 13,123 feet (4,000 meters) above sea level. The Hengduan mountain chain, Qilianshan Mountains and Kunlunshan Mountain range are the dividing line between this step and the second one. The peak that is the highest in the world, Everest, sits at 29,015 feet (8,844.43 meters). This is also called "the Roof of the World."

On the ladder elevation, the second step consists of plateaus and basins, the majority of which are 3,280 feet (1,000 meters) up to 6,561 feet (2,000 meters) high above sea level. This step is divided by the Wu, Taihang, Xuefeng, and Daxing'an Mountains. The plateaus include the Sichuan Basin, Junngar Basin, Tarim Basin, and more.

The Zhangjiajie National Forest Park is a unique forested area located near Zhangjiajie City in Hunan Province.

The last and third step is abundant in broad plains, but also full of foothills and lower mountains that are frequently higher than 1,640 feet (500 meters) above sea level. Here is where the most well-known plains are found, including the Middle-Lower Yangtze Plain, the North China Plain, and the Northeast China Plain, which run from north to south. These fertile and well-cultivated lands are known for producing extremely abundant crops.

While the physical features of China are as described above, the people usually divide China into four different regions: the Northwest, North, South, and the Qinghai-Tibetan areas. Due to the geographical differences, the residents of each of these regions have very distinctive customs and lifestyles.

China has more than 50,000 rivers that have drainage areas larger than 38 square miles (100 square kilometers), with over 1,500 exceeding 386 square miles (1,000 square kilometers) in area.

Learn more about the geography of China by watching this 11-minute educational video. Scan the QR code with your phone to watch!

The Yangtze is the longest river in Asia.

About two-thirds of the countryside is considered mountainous. The ranges typically run from the east to the west and from the northeast to the southeast. There are some mountains that seem to reach all the way to the sky, while others are much lower and offer picturesque scenery.

The Climate

The climate of China varies greatly from one region to another. In the northeast portion of the country, the summers are extremely dry and hot and the winters are extremely cold. In the central and northern regions of China, there are frequent bouts of rain combined with hot summer months and cold winters. For the southeast region, rainfall is plentiful and the area has a semi-tropical climate in the summers, with cool (not cold) winters. Flooding is common in the western, southern, and central regions, and in general, the country experiences frequent earthquakes.

Because of the geographic position of the country, both southern and eastern China are significantly affected by monsoons, and they have a climate that is similar to other countries that are prone to being affected by monsoons. In the western portion of China, there are two different types of climates. The majority of the regions are dry and cold during the winter months and have a rainy and warm climate during the summer.

Due to its diverse terrain and topographical conditions, China's climate is considered complicated and can be quite diverse from one region to another. For example, in the northern section of the Heilongjiang province there is an extremely long winter, but there isn't a summer. The year-round average temperature of China is 53° Fahrenheit (11° Celsius), with the highest temperature reaching 88° F (31° Celsius) and the lowest dropping to 14° F (-10° Celsius). The hottest months of the year are July and August and the coldest months are January and December.

Some regions in China have very long and harsh winters.

When it comes to rain, rainfall is generally regular each year, with approximately 66 days a year that experience some rainfall. Precipitation increases from the southeast to the northwest because the eastern areas are much more influenced by the summer monsoon season, which brings both rainfall and vapor in the form of fog and mist.

Flora and Fauna

China is home to some of the most diverse wildlife in the entire world. In fact, there are more than 2,000 species of land-based vertebrates, which represent over 10 percent of the entire world's population. Additionally, 1,189 species of birds and almost 500 animal species—along with 320 species of reptiles and 210 species of amphibians—call China their home. There are many rare wild species that are only found in the country of China. Some of these include the Chinese alligator, the Chinese river dolphin, the takin, white-lipped deer, the golden monkey, and the giant panda.

The Giant Panda

The giant panda is a black and white species of bear that lives in the temperate-zone bamboo forests located in central China. They are one of the most recognized and rarest animals in the entire world. Due to this, the giant panda has come to symbolize the risk of all endangered species and the conservation efforts in place to try to save each one.

The giant panda lives in several of the mountain ranges in central China. While they once inhabited the lowland areas, forest clearing, farming, and other types of development have restricted the giant panda's living space to just the mountainous regions. They now live in coniferous and broadleaf forests where quite a bit of bamboo is found, at elevations ranging between 5,000 (1,524 meters) and 10,000 feet (3,048 meters) above sea level.

The giant panda is considered one of the national treasures of China and these cute, bamboo-eating animals live in the desolate mountain areas of the Shaanxi, Gansu, and Sichuan provinces. The panda is called a "living fossil" because it is considered a remnant species—one that thrived during the period of the glaciers and is still available to see today.

The country of China is home to 7,000 species of different woody plants, with 2,800 of these being arboreal. There are several that are only found in China: the Eucommia, Fujian cypress, Taiwan flousiana, golden larch, China fir, silver fir, cathaya, China cypress, and the metasequoia. The metasequoia tree can grow to be 114 feet (35 meters tall)—or higher! It was most commonly found in Europe, North America, and East Asia more than 100 million years ago and was thought to have become extinct during the last glacial period. However, China discovered over 1,000 of these trees at the Sichuan-Hubei border in 1941. It was considered one of the biggest and most important botanical discoveries that occurred in the twentieth century. After 1949, individual metasequoia plants were sent to other countries around the world in hopes of repopulating the species.

China is famous for its bamboo forests. Bamboo is the panda's main diet.

RESEARCH PROJECT

Write a one-page essay on how climate change has affected the climate, flora, and fauna in China.

TEXT-DEPENDENT QUESTIONS

1. What ocean borders China?

2. What tree was thought to be extinct until it was rediscovered in 1941?

3. Name a rare animal species that is found in China.

The Jiaohe ancient ruins near Turpan are in the Xinjiang Uyghur region. They date to 108 BCE.

WORDS TO UNDERSTAND

dynasties: sequences of rulers from the same family or group

feudal society: a system of government where peasants received a piece of land in exchange for serving as a soldier in times of war

Great Leap Forward: an effort by the Communist Party of China to quickly industrialize the nation under the rule of Mao Zedong

CHAPTER 2

THE GOVERNMENT & HISTORY OF CHINA

China is one of the oldest civilizations still existing on earth. Its long history has captured the imagination of people throughout the centuries. The country went from being a nation of hunter-gatherers to farmers, and finally to being ruled by various **dynasties** throughout the ages, some of which imposed brutal laws. Others were more relaxed. In 2019, China is an economic power ruled by a Communist government that promotes trade and has made China into an economic superpower.

Prehistoric China

In the beginning, the people of China survived by hunting wild game and fish and gathering plants, nuts, and berries. Chinese archaeologists have found ancient stone tools that may have been used for hunting. Many of these tools contain engravings that suggest the original Chinese people had language during prehistoric times.

By 5000 BCE, the Chinese began farming. In southern China, rice was cultivated, while northern China grew another grain called "millet." There is evidence that dogs and pigs were domesticated at this time and by 3000 BCE, the Chinese had also domesticated cattle and sheep. Around 2300 BCE, horses were introduced.

Terra-cotta army: Discover the greatest archaeological find of the twentieth century with BBC News.

Farmers learned to make pottery during this prehistoric time, along with baskets, woven cloth, and ritual objects. In 2500 BCE, the wheel was invented in China.

As Chinese society became more advanced, by 2000 BCE they had learned to make items from bronze. The first items forged were used as weapons, since tribal war became commonplace. This was most likely due to the growing gap between rich and poor among the Chinese. By around 1700 BCE, vessels were being made out of bronze. Other tools, such as plows, spades, and sickles were made of stone or wood.

There is also evidence that the Chinese began conducting human sacrifices at this time. The sacrificed bodies were buried under building foundations. Fortune-telling was also practiced, and by 1300 BCE, China was producing silk from the silkworm.

The Dynasties of China
The Shang Dynasty

The first dynasty to rule China was the Shang Dynasty. They were polytheists whose most revered god was called Di. It was during this time that the Chinese began the ancient tradition of ancestor worship—the belief that dead ancestors can influence the life of a person. For this reason, the Chinese left offerings for their ancestors to encourage them to help their living relatives.

The Shang Dynasty was the first to build Chinese cities, with the capital, Zhengzhou,

A dragon-shaped gong from the Shang Dynasty.

This modern sculpture on the Yellow River represents emperors Yan and Huang who were early rulers of China.

surrounded by walls for protection from enemies. They also built palaces and temples and participated in the slave trade. Typically, it was prisoners of war who were taken as slaves.

Human sacrifice continued in the Shang Dynasty. In fact, when a Shang emperor died, his servants and slaves were expected to commit suicide in order to accompany the ruler into the afterlife. If they didn't commit suicide, they were killed.

In 1022 BCE, the Shang Dynasty was overthrown by the Zhou, who created a dynasty of their own.

The Zhou Dynasty

This dynasty ruled until 221 BCE and is credited with creating a **feudal society**, which helped keep control over a population that was spanning a large geographic area. Citizens were given land and titles in exchange for serving as soldiers and providing chariots during war, and these lands and positions

Confucianism Philosophy

The philosophy of the Zhou Dynasty was created by Confucius, who called for children to honor their parents. He said that everyone should honor their ancestors and accept their own position in life. This philosophy also embraced the ideas that all people should have consideration for others, and to have moderation in all things. Women were taught to be submissive to their fathers and husbands and to value humility.

Although Confucius never wrote any books himself, his followers collected his teachings, which survived and influenced China for 2,000 years.

The Taoist Zhongyue Temple near Zhengzhou City. Parts of the site date back to the Qin Dynasty.

became hereditary, being passed down to the sons. A lord ruled over the land while the peasants, who were at the bottom of this feudal hierarchy, worked the land to produce food. The peasants farmed their own plot of land along with a communal plot whose yield went directly to the lord of the land.

By 600 BCE, the Chinese had begun to use coins as currency. Therefore, some peasants chose to pay taxes to their lord rather than produce food. While slavery flourished under the Shang Dynasty, there were very few slaves during the Zhou Dynasty.

Taoism Under the Zhou Dynasty

The Tao is a force behind everything—humans and nature alike—and the belief system called "Taoism" is a belief in Tao and is also known as "the way" or "dao." The Taoist believes in non-action and teaches that humility and compassion are the way to live a good life.

Other Chinese Beliefs During the Zhou Dynasty

The I Ching was developed, which is a form of divination. The philosophy of yin and yang also appeared at this time. This is the belief that everything is made from two opposites: Yin as the feminine, gentle part and yang as the masculine, hard part. Acupuncture was also invented under the Zhou Dynasty. This dynasty, however, began to decline in 771 BCE and was conquered by a state named Qin.

The Qin Dynasty

Qin Shi Huangdi is considered the first emperor of China. The benefits he brought to China included a standard of weights and measurements and a standard version of

The world famous terra-cotta army is part of the mausoleum of the first Qin Emperor. It is a UNESCO World Heritage Site located in Xian.

China's most famous landmark, the Great Wall, dates back to the Qin Dynasty.

Chinese writing. Those who opposed him were sent to work as laborers on the Great Wall or buried alive. To control the enormous population of China, the Qin Dynasty divided the nation into thirty-four areas called "commanderies," with a governor ruling over each. The governors also had the responsibility to build roads and irrigation canals.

When Qin Shi Huangdi died, his body was buried in a tomb that contained 7,000 terra-cotta soldiers. This tomb was unearthed in 1974 and became famous as a fascinating archaeological discovery. However, fierce punishments and heavy taxes had burdened the Chinese people, and rebellions broke out. Once the last emperor of the Qin Dynasty was executed, this gave rise to the Han Dynasty.

The Han Dynasty

During this era, Chinese society really began to take shape. The Han Dynasty is considered a brilliant time for Chinese civilization. The watermill and chain pump were invented during this time.

The first emperor of the Han Dynasty was Gaozi. China began to fully adopt the Confucian philosophies that continued with Gaozi's successors. By 124 BCE, Chinese scholars were studying Confucian texts such as The Book of Changes, The Book of Rites, The Book of Documents, The Book of Songs, and the Book of Spring and Autumn Annals. After studying, they took an exam. If they passed, they were given high official positions.

Xi'an was once called Chang'an. It was an ancient city of the Han Dynasty.

Like the dynasty before them, the Han Dynasty imposed heavy taxes as agriculture improved and the population grew. Ships brought silk to trade with the Roman Empire. Paper was invented during this time and Buddhism was beginning to take hold, along with the art of Feng Shui.

China Divided

The fall of the Han Dynasty resulted in three kingdoms being formed. However, these kingdoms ended up fighting each other and the Wul kingdom eventually conquered all of China in 280 CE, bringing peace to a divided nation. However, when the rulers allowed the Xiongnu people to live within China's walls with the hope of assimilation, their plan backfired. The Xiongnu overran the north of China, which was then split into rival kingdoms, all with non-Chinese rulers. This era is known as the Sixteen Kingdoms.

The Chinese emperors to the south tried to overtake the north, but were unable to do so. In the fourth century CE, a people from Turkey called the Torba began taking over China in the north and conquered it by 386 CE. The Torba went on to assimilate north China, absorbing all of Chinese culture, including the style of dress and writing.

In 581 CE, a Chinese general was able to overtake the north and start a short-lived Sui Dynasty. After the second emperor of this dynasty died, China fell into warring chaos. One bright spot was that Buddhism grew and many temples and monasteries were built, making Buddhism the official religion of China.

The Tang Dynasty

Considered one of the greatest eras in China's history, the Tang Dynasty lasted from 618 to 907 CE. The arts flourished, including poetry. Outside influences also began to make their way into China, including the religions of Islam and Christianity. Gunpowder was invented and used for bombs to break through enemy gates.

During the middle of the eighth century, the Tang Dynasty began to decline with the defeat by the Arabs. The result was that China lost control of central Asia.

Although Buddhism was very popular during this time, the Tang Dynasty resented that fact that monks did not pay taxes and used precious copper to make bells, chimes, and statues. With a shortage of copper for coins, Emperor Wuzong declared that all monasteries be taken over for their copper components and that all monks return to civilian life. By 907 CE, the Tang Dynasty was no more due to rebellion and war.

Other Dynasties of China

In 907 CE, China was once again split into states. From this time on, five short-lived dynasties ruled. These were the Quidan Liao Dynasty, the Song Dynasty, the Yuan Dynasty, the Ming Dynasty, and the Qing Dynasty.

Wu Zetian

Wu Zetian was the only woman to rule as Empress of China. Under the Tang Dynasty, her rule lasted from 660 to 705 BCE. She was not born into royalty, but her family was wealthy. She achieved her rule by marrying Emperor Gaozong. After he suffered a debilitating stroke in 660 BCE, Wu took over as empress.

She is most known for improving China's public education system, reforming agriculture, and changing the tax system. Those officials whose peasants produced the most food were taxed less than others. Wu also oversaw the creation of farming manuals, built irrigation ditches, and redistributed land among her citizens so that everyone had an equal share of land to farm.

Opium Wars

In the early 1800s, Britain introduced opium to China. This addictive drug was frowned upon by the rulers, who demanded that Britain hand over all the opium they were smuggling. They agreed, but then sent a fleet to block Chinese ports. Finally, a treaty was negotiated in 1841 to stop the opium wars.

The Revolution

During the 1900s, the Chinese government began to resist outside influences on their nation. They didn't like the interference of Christian missionaries and other Western effects on their society, which eventually led to China's modern rebellion called the Cultural Revolution in the 1960s and 1970s. The Chinese people began to call for a new order, one that didn't rely on past philosophies or on outside influences. That desire gave rise to the decision to apply communism to the government in 1921, which remains to this day.

The Chinese Communist Party was created on the ideas of Karl Marx. One of the founders of the party, Mao Zedong, went on to become its head. He led a

Mao Zedong declares the founding of the modern People's Republic of China on October 1, 1949.

peasant uprising in 1927 that overtook China's government and installed a Communist military state after ridding the country of all outside influence.

Modern China

Under Communist rule, China started down a road of industrialization with an iron hand. Those who didn't agree with Mao were severely punished. In 1958, he implemented what is known as **"The Great Leap Forward,"** a plan to create community agriculture that was combined with other areas of commerce with the intention of moving China forward. Unfortunately, the arrangement didn't work and led to a lack of food that killed millions of people.

In 1966, Mao created the Cultural Revolution. It removed all outside influences, along with all past beliefs held by the Chinese. The Red Guard was formed to make

Red books dating back to Mao's rule contained quotes from the leader. Most Chinese people owned one.

sure everyone in China was moving toward a new China—one without old beliefs, religions, and outside influence. When Mao died, the Red Guard was dismantled. China headed in a new direction, toward a market economy.

In 2019, China is a success story. After centuries of fighting and living under dynasties and the tight rule of Mao, the Chinese economy began to grow rapidly. Now it seems that nearly everything is made in China, from electronics and clothing to toys, and everything else in between. China is expected to have the world's largest economy by the year 2040. As of 2018, its enormous population totaled 1.37 billion people.

RESEARCH PROJECT

Write a brief report on one of China's dynasties.

TEXT-DEPENDENT QUESTIONS

1. What is Confucianism?

2. Why did Mao want to remove all outside influences from China?

3. What can be attributed to China's modern growth?

minority: a group in society distinguished from, and less dominant than, the more numerous majority

powerhouse: a person or thing having unusual strength or energy

socialism: a system by which ownership and control of production and distribution is owned by the community as a whole

THE CHINESE ECONOMY

While the Chinese economy flourished with agriculture in the past, today it is a **powerhouse** of modern enterprise. China churns out a massive number of items for trade with various countries. As of 2018, China boasts second place when it comes to the world's strongest economy. The number one spot goes to the United States, while Canada is in spot eleven. China is the world's biggest exporter and has the world's largest economy. Unfortunately, it also has a low per capita income compared to the world average. One reason for this is the large population of the country.

However, China's economic freedom score is only 57.8, which puts it at the 110th freest economy in the world. In contrast, Japan was determined to be the thirtieth freest economy in the index for 2018. While the economy is not entirely free, it has had tremendous benefits at home and abroad. But there is little reform taking place to change China's economic freedom score. The nation's leaders appear to be shying away from liberalism and are instead becoming less open to imports and investments.

Socialism in the People's Republic of China

With the rise of the Communist Party in China, the focus has been on using **socialism** to create an economic superpower that raises the standard of living across the country. Known as the socialist market economy (SME), this economic model is a system based on the predominance of state-owned enterprises and public ownership within its market economy. The term was first coined in 1992 by the 14th National Congress of the Communist Party of China.

The Great Hall of the People is a state building in Beijing. It is used for legislative and ceremonial activities by the government of China.

An engineer working in an oil refinery in Jiujiang in the northwest of Jiangxi Province.

The Economy of China

Gross Domestic Product (GDP):
$23.1 trillion USD

Industries:
manufacturing, services, agriculture

Agriculture:
fruit, vegetables, rice, soybeans, corn, peanuts, millet, pork

Export Commodities:
electrical and other machinery and manufactured goods

Export Partners:
United States, Hong Kong, Japan, South Korea

Import Commodities:
mineral fuels including oil, iron ore, copper and copper ore, oil seeds, and coal

Import Partners:
United States, South Korea, Japan, Germany, and Australia

Currency:
Renminbi

Source: www.cia.gov 2017

Taxes

In China, the top personal income tax rate is 45 percent, while the top corporate rate is 25 percent. Other taxes include real estate taxes. Overall, the tax burden is 17.5 percent of the total domestic income. These taxes give the government the money it needs for social services, roads, and other public works.

Pollution in China

China's pollution is extremely serious and accounts for many early deaths in the country. Overall, the problem costs the Chinese economy $38 billion USD a year. Most of the pollution is caused by factories, diesel engine motor vehicles, and lax environmental laws.

Property Rights

Compared to other countries, China scores low when it comes to property rights. For example, the state owns all urban land, while citizens only own the buildings on top of the land. In rural China, land is owned collectively by villages, which follows the Communist model.

Labor Force

In 2016, China's labor force was made up of 776 million workers, which is about 71 percent of the total population. Labor is used in factories, agriculture, government positions, and in other areas.

Economic Sectors

There are three major areas that make up China's economy: manufacturing, the service industry, and agriculture. Manufacturing is the biggest income generator. China makes and sells more manufactured goods than any other nation in the world. In fact, China is the world leader in many types of exported goods. These include electronics, ships, rail cars, steel, iron, aluminum, chemicals, cement, toys, aircraft, and more. They make more air-conditioning units than any other country, as well as more personal computers, cell phones, and other electronic devices.

China has a healthy services sector. In fact, 43 percent of the labor force can be found working in this sector. Since 2015, with the development of shopping malls across China, the services sector has exploded. People have money to spend and they need services to help them spend it! This includes tourists visiting China, who also have money to spend. Large foreign companies, such as IBM and Microsoft, have also been settling down in China, which is boosting the growth of the telecommunications industry.

Skilled workers attach microchips to circuit boards in a Jiangxi factory.

As of 2018, there are more than 300 million farmers in China, which sets the world record for any other nation. China mainly grows rice for export, but also produces tobacco, potatoes, wheat, millet, pork, peanuts, corn, soybeans, tea, and fruits and vegetables for export. Unfortunately, however, Chinese farms remain severely underproductive per capita when compared to other farming nations like the United States. Part of this is due to an unfavorable climate. But next-door in North Korea, the climate is the same, yet their farmers produce 40 percent more crops than Chinese farms. Other issues include the fact that many farms are state-controlled and farmers cannot get credit to purchase farmland and equipment, two driving factors that limit the amount of food produced.

Farming in China is not as productive as in the United States. These Chinese women are planting rice.

Learn how China's transportation system is the best in the world.

China's population is 1.4 billion as of 2018. Its Gross Domestic Product (GDP) is $23.1 trillion USD, with 6.9 percent growth. Its GDP per capita is $8,826.99 USD. The unemployment rate is 4.6 percent and inflation is 2 percent. Like many nations around the world, there are those who earn more and those who earn less in China.

Transportation

As China's economy began to improve in the late 1970s, so did the modes of transportation. These, however, vary by location. Cities and coastal areas have more developed means of transportation, while the rural areas wait to catch up. China is a huge country, so the easiest way to travel long distances is by railway. There are many roads, airports, and railways throughout China for travel. In some cities, people who can afford it even choose to travel by helicopter to avoid traffic!

China's extensive railway system is the longest in the world at 15,534 miles (25,000 kilometers) of high-speed rail line. China is also seeing a major boost of aircraft in the country, with international airports in Beijing and Shanghai. China also boasts thirty-four metro systems, bus transport, and personal vehicle travel.

Energy

When it comes to wind turbines and solar panels, China is the largest manufacturer of both. China's energy comes from renewable sources (7 percent) such as hydropower. However, a large portion of its energy (70 percent) comes from coal, which is used to create a large percentage of the nation's electricity.

Economic Problems

Even though China makes and sells more manufactured goods than any other nation in the world, its financial problems are many. First of all, the Chinese debt load is $1.6 trillion USD—and doesn't show any signs of decreasing. Another factor facing China is pollution. Because of pollution, the nation is having a hard time recruiting talented foreigners to live and work in the country. Also, a high level of poverty among the millions of rural inhabitants is a serious problem.

Minorities

The ethnic minorities in China consist of the non-Han Chinese population, along with fifty-four other recognized **minority** groups, such as Jews, Tuvan, Oirat, and various Taiwanese groups. These groups make up 8.49 percent of the population and are collectively referred to as "Zhonghua Minzu."

China's central business district in Beijing.

RESEARCH PROJECT

Write a brief report on the evolution of China's economy.

TEXT-DEPENDENT QUESTIONS

1. What is the main source of China's economy?

2. How is pollution hurting China's economy?

3. How did China's economy grow so quickly?

Yao people can trace their ancestry back 2,000 years. Today, they are an ethnic minority in China.

elite: persons of the highest class in a society; they receive the choicest or best of anything in society, from goods to jobs, and such privileges are restricted only to them

go underground: be or go into hiding; keep out of sight, as for protection and safety; to start working or meeting in secret

immigration: the act of coming to a country of which one is not a native, usually for permanent residence

CITIZENS OF CHINA—PEOPLE, CUSTOMS & CULTURE

China is home to 1.38 billion people, making it the world's most populated country and the second largest country in Asia after Russia. The population density is 375 people per square mile, or 145 people per square kilometer and the nation contains many ethnicities, languages, and customs.

Ethnicities

Altogether, there are fifty-six ethnic groups in China. The Han Chinese make up the largest ethnicity in China, accounting for 91.59 percent of the country's entire population. The Han's total population is 1.6 billion and they live in almost every part of the country, but mainly the Han live in the areas of the Yellow River, Yangtze River, Pearl River, and along the Songliao Plain. Not only do the Han make up the largest ethnic group in China, they are also the largest ethnic group in the entire world.

The remaining ethnic groups make up 8.41 percent of the rest of the population and can be found throughout China's different regions, although the greatest number of other ethnic groups can be found in the Yunnan province, with the second largest ethnic group being the Zhuang with a population of more than 16 million. Many ethnic groups throughout China live in their own individual communities. However, they have been able to create positive relationships with each other over the years.

Other ethnic groups that make up China include: the Achang, Bai, Bonan, Bouyei, Blang, Dai, Daur, Deang, Dong, Dongxiang, Dulong, Ewenki, Gaoshan, Gelao, Hani, Hezhe, Hui, Jing, Jingpo, Jinuo, Kazak, Kirgiz, Korean, Lahu, Li, Lisu, Luoba, Manchu, Maonan, Menba, Miao, Mongolian, Mulao, Naxi, Nu, Oroqen, Ozbek, Pumi, Qiang, Russian, Salar, She, Shui, Tajik, Tatar, Tibetan, Tu, Tujia, Uigur, Wa, Xibe, Yao, Yi, Yugur, and Zhuang.

Naxi women in traditional dress performing a dance in the city of Lijiang.

Learn about China's ethnic minorities in this video.

Education and Sports

China has the largest education system in the world. The government invests 4 percent of the total GDP into education and has made it compulsory for Chinese citizens to finish at least nine years of education. Furthermore, many international students choose to study in China. In 2018, for example, there were over 450,000 foreign students studying in China.

Teaching is a highly respected profession in China and the government consistently offers teacher development training. The government is also working to improve the country's curriculum. Education in China can be traced back to the sixteenth century BCE. However, during this time, education was reserved only for the **elite**.

The Chinese love to play sports, with their favorites being running, table tennis, badminton, soccer, and basketball. Running is considered the trendiest sport in

China for recreational athletes between the ages of thirty-six and forty-five. Although seen as a hobby sport, the Chinese take running marathons very seriously. In fact, there are typically over 100 marathons run in China each year.

Winter sports such as skiing are also taking hold in China, especially since they will be hosting the Winter Olympics in 2022.

Food and Drink

The term "Chinese food" is known throughout the world. However, authentic Chinese food is typically only found in China. In other locations, diners are generally served Americanized versions that are not accurate.

China's cuisine is diverse, with a variety of dishes found throughout the different regions of the country. However, a Chinese meal is typically made up of two main ingredients: a starch (noodles, rice), and a vegetable or meat, including fish. The main ingredients of a meal depend upon the area. For example, those who live in northern China eat mainly wheat-based noodles, while in southern China, people tend to consume more rice.

The Chinese use chopsticks to eat, rather than forks and knives, because these Western utensils are considered weapons and should never be used to eat with. Although in modern times, some Chinese do use Western utensils for eating. Another interesting fact about Chinese food is that it is served on a communal plate that everyone eats from.

Tea is the most popular drink in China and comes in many varieties. Tea is said to help with digestion and is used to treat ailments and other conditions.

Immigrants

Immigration to China remains small. Most immigrants have been of Chinese nationality. For example, many Chinese have chosen to move back to China since the economy has improved. Foreign workers are encouraged to immigrate to China, especially in the fields of aviation and education. However, these workers are not

Winter sports are becoming popular in China. In 2022, China will be hosting the Winter Olympics for the first time.

considered immigrants as they maintain their respective country citizenship and are only in China on a work visa, which does not allow for Chinese citizenship.

Language

China has 297 languages spoken throughout the country among its fifty-six ethnic groups. The most popular language spoken is Mandarin Chinese, with over 955 million citizens speaking it. The official language of China is called Standard Chinese. It is based on Mandarin but has other features of various dialects included. For example, many Chinese use the Beijing dialect to pronounce many Mandarin

Chinese words. Other languages spoken in China include Cantonese, Wu Chinese, Fuzhou, and Hokkien. Foreign languages spoken in China include English (10 million speakers) and Portuguese.

Religion in China

Religious observance in China is growing, mainly due to the country's economic boom and swift modernization. Many Chinese are turning to Christianity or going back to traditional Chinese religions. The Chinese State allows for religious observance by individuals; however, many face repression and persecution, which forces them to **go underground** to worship.

According to Article 36 of the Chinese constitution, citizens are free to enjoy religious beliefs. On paper, the country bans discrimination for religious beliefs but it

The Chongsheng Monastery in Dali is one of the largest Buddhist centers in Southeast Asia.

Church of the Saviour is a historic Catholic church in Beijing.

also bans evangelism. Furthermore, while religious groups can certainly possess property and publish religious literature, this is tightly controlled by the state. As of 2019, China only recognizes five religions in the country: Buddhism, Taoism, Islam, Catholicism, and Protestantism. Practicing any other faith is strictly forbidden.

The Chinese government has officially registered about 100 million religious believers, which make up 10 percent of the total population.

Underground Churches in China

The Communist Party tried to eradicate religion in China but failed. In 2019, there are more Christians than Communists in China. Many of these Christians worship together in caves and other secluded spots in rural areas to avoid being harassed or jailed by government officials.

Chinese opera is a form of musical theater with roots going back to the early periods.

However, it is suggested that this number is actually larger since many people go underground to practice their choice of worship to avoid persecution. Those religious groups that are registered are closely monitored by the government to prevent protests or other interference that could disrupt the public order.

Furthermore, China has one of the largest populations of religious prisoners.

The Arts: Architecture, Painting, Music, and Literature

The Chinese love art. They have been involved in the arts for centuries and excel in each form. Chinese art includes painting, sculpture, the performing arts, and more.

China has a long history of developing art. Cave paintings dating back centuries can be found in China's mountainous regions. These include scenes about nature, people, and animals. As the Chinese moved forward from living as hunter-gatherers, they developed the painting skills that are still seen in modern times. The central theme of nature and harmony with the surrounding world remained as this art form progressed.

The performing arts are also found in China. From Kung Fu to folk dances and even opera, China has a long history of performing arts. Singing and acting have also emerged as art forms in China. Other performing arts include Chinese Shadow Play, the Chinese Dragon Dance, and traditional Chinese music.

The Chinese are also masters of craft projects such as embroidery, Chinese bonsai, Chinese lanterns, and more. The nation's people are also well-known for their sculptures, pottery, jade carvings, and calligraphy writing.

RESEARCH PROJECT

Write a one page report on the arts of China.

TEXT-DEPENDENT QUESTIONS

1. Are the Chinese able to openly express their religion? Why or why not?

2. What are some of the most important arts practiced in China?

3. Why has immigration to China been slow?

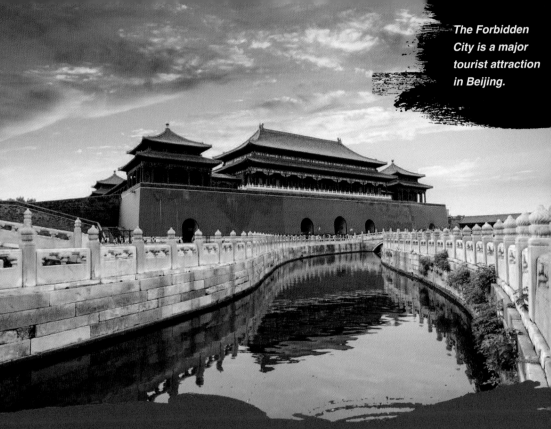

The Forbidden City is a major tourist attraction in Beijing.

WORDS TO UNDERSTAND

Lunar Chinese New Year: an important Chinese festival celebrated at the turn of the traditional lunisolar Chinese calendar

Maglev Train: "maglev" is short for "magnetic levitation," which means the trains will float over a guideway using the basic principles of magnets to replace the old steering wheel and track trains

Pinyin Method: the official system for translating Chinese characters (毛泽东, Mao Tse-tung) into the Latin alphabet (Mao Zedong) to teach Standard Chinese

CHAPTER 5

FAMOUS CITIES OF CHINA

China has one of the longest continuous civilizations of any country on earth. With some Chinese culture and history records dating back to 3000 BCE, China offers history and beauty in its culture as no other country can. In the past, war and farming dominated the Chinese landscape, but in modern times, China has built a number of large cities filled with factories, entertainment, housing, transportation systems, and more. These cities now define modern Chinese culture.

Beijing (Peking)

Beijing is the capital of China and is the third largest city in the world. Some people may still know the capital as Peking; however, the name was changed when the **Pinyin Method** converted Mandarin into the Roman alphabet. Beijing has wonderful attractions including the Forbidden City, the Temple of Heaven, and the Summer Palace.

The Forbidden City is located in central Beijing and was the former imperial palace starting from the Ming Dynasty to the end of the Qing Dynasty (1420–1912). The Forbidden City complex was home to the past emperors and their family members during this time era. They had ceremonies for special occasions and also had most of their political Chinese government meetings there.

Visit and learn more about the Great Wall of China, which has an average of 10 million visitors yearly.

Beacon and watch towers

The complex has 980 buildings and sits on over 180 acres. The city was built by over 1 million men, including more than 100,000 craftsmen, and it took fourteen years to build. In modern time, it is considered a beautiful palace museum full of art and history. It still maintains beautiful traditional Chinese architecture and has the largest collection of preserved ancient wooden structures in the world.

The Temple of Heaven was built in 1420 CE and is located in southern Beijing. Since the time of the Ming Dynasty (1200s–1300s CE), many emperors came to the temple to pray for good harvests and then came back to thank the heavens for their crops. Inside the temple are three sets of circular columns. One set has four columns that represent the four seasons, the second set has twelve columns representing the months of the year, and the last set has twenty-four columns representing the harvests or plants that were grown at that time.

The Summer Palace is located 9 miles northwest of downtown Beijing. The Summer Palace is the largest and most preserved royal park in China. The park shows off some historic Chinese horticulture plants while displaying famous landscape views at the same time.

The garden was made in 1750 CE and was a beautiful place for members of the royal family to bring their friends to enjoy the gardens and scenery. The royal family loved the palace and grounds so much that the family decided to move there toward the end of the Qing Dynasty. Unfortunately, the gardens were burned down by the British-French Allied Force at the end of the Second Opium War.

The Summer Palace was a popular place for members of the royal family. It is beautifully preserved, as are the grounds.

The Bird's Nest is China's national stadium. It was built for the Beijing summer Olympic Games held in 2008.

According to Chinese history, the original name for this beautiful garden was Qingyi Palace (Garden of Clear Ripples) before the fire. The park was renamed "Yiheyuan" (the Summer Palace) after it was re-created in 1888.

Beijing is also one of communism's strongest footholds in the world in 2018. Some of the Communist policies are still used by believers, but others have abandoned the ways of communism and are becoming more involved in newer common theories, such as capitalism.

Considered one of the famous Seven Wonders of the World, the Great Wall of China is around 13,130 miles (21,130 kilometers) long and crosses over nine provinces throughout northern China. The wall is so long that it would take someone eighteen months to walk from one end to the other. A popular myth says you can see the wall from the moon because it's so big, but that's not true. The wall was finally completed in 1644 CE when the last ruler of the Ming Dynasty was overthrown, after it was worked on for over 2,000 years. There are many towers along the wall for people to worship the god of war, Guandi. Many Chinese people also believe that the wall is a personification of the Chinese dragon.

The shopping streets in Beijing are popular with locals and tourists alike.

Shanghai is a modern and vibrant city. It is the largest urban area in China and a global financial center.

Shanghai

Most people have heard of the great big city of Shanghai. Whether through famous movies, books, or businesses, Shanghai has definitely made a name for itself. With a population of over 20 million people, Shanghai is the largest city in China. It was voted as the most attractive city for the fourth time in 2016 for its living environment and foreign policies. The people of Shanghai are determined to keep this city in the top spot.

Shanghai became one of the largest and busiest container ports in the world during the 2000s and 2010s. The city opened its docks to wholeheartedly become involved in the trade industry. There are many different kinds of products made in China that are sold throughout the world. Many businesses are booming because of the shipping success, and more businesses pop up every day that hope to share the same success. This provides extra jobs for the millions of middle to lower class people that live in Shanghai or nearby.

The world's longest metro system travels below Shanghai with 393 stations while traveling over 400 miles (643 kilometers) of track, including multiple tunnels

Tourist boats on the canals of the Shanghai Zhujiajiao Water Town, an ancient place near Shanghai.

throughout. The trains travel to many different attractions throughout the city, and also provide transportation to the residential areas. The fastest train in Shanghai is the **Maglev Train**. This train travels from the Shanghai Pudong Airport to the Longyang Road Metro Station at an operating speed of 300 kph, which is around 180 mph. Traveling the distance of 30 kilometers on the Maglev Train only takes around 30 minutes. Its maximum speed has been recorded at 267 mph (430 kph), which is nearly the speed airplanes need to take off. Pudong and Hongqiao International airports have a combination of over 110 million travelers annually.

Shanghai currently has the world's second largest skyscraper (2018), with a recorded height of 137 floors and standing tall at 2,073 feet (631 meters), with a

The Shanghai Maglev Train is also known as the Shanghai Transrapid.

The Huxinting Teahouse in the Yu Garden, in the old city of Shanghai, is a popular tourist destination.

otal floor area of 4,090,285 square feet (380,000 square meters)! The completion of he Shanghai Tower took seven years, starting in 2008, and was finished in 2015. Jp near the top is a twisted section of 120 degrees, which is intended to reduce vind gusts up to 24 percent. The tower is made up of nine cylindrical buildings stacked on top of each other, all enclosed by an inner wall of glass. The nine sections provide different indoor zones for visitors. Each has its own restaurants, atriums, gardens, and of course, beautiful views of the city below.

Hong Kong

Traveling to Hong Kong for a family vacation will not disappoint anyone. There is so nuch to do in Hong Kong for everyone at any time of the day or night. Between the nany shopping spots, the exquisite mouthwatering cuisines of different international

A view of Hong Kong and Victoria Harbour. Hong Kong is one of the world's most densely populated areas.

foods, and the parks, temples, and museums to explore, visitors won't run out of things to do.

Hong Kong is a combination of the east and west parts of China, blending both the people and their cultures together. Hong Kong also has cultural influences of Cantonese, Mandarin, British, and communities such as Hakka, Fujian, and Shanghainese. All the different cultures are special in their own way, yet live together in harmony and understanding.

Compared to Shanghai's metro system, Hong Kong's transit system is even better, and is considered one of the best in the world. Even though buses and train cars are crowded because of the city's 7–8 million people who live and work there, public transportation is the best way to commute. Luckily it is relatively inexpensive, which encourages people to use the system and reduces the number of cars on the roads.

Hong Kong Island steals the attention away from the total 263 islands of Hong Kong. Some of the other popular islands like Lantau, Cheung Chau, and Lamma are accessible by ferry, but most of the islands are inhabitable and unreachable.

Many hotels and apartment buildings do not have a fourth floor in Hong Kong. Not having a fourth floor is common because the number four sounds like the word "death" in Chinese and is considered unlucky. In the United States, some buildings do not have a thirteenth floor because many believe it is an unlucky number.

Chinese New Year is celebrated much like Christmas is celebrated in the United States. Most tourist attractions close down for the first day of the **Lunar Chinese New Year**, while shops and restaurants close down for a couple of days so they too can participate in the fun and festivities. During the New Year celebration, the city of Hong Kong is decorated with rich colors of red, gold, and green that hang

The Tsim Sha Tsui area is a very popular shopping destination in Hong Kong.

down from the tall skyscrapers all over the city. Down on the streets they are decorated with colored ribbons that hang on every street lamppost and building available.

The flower markets in Victoria Park are always filled with brightly colored and decorated people wanting to buy some bright, beautiful flowers. The flowers are known to be considered good luck when given to a friend or family member when visiting them for the New Year's traditional meal, which typically includes chicken or fish.

One of the important things the Chinese like to do while celebrating the Chinese New Year is to visit their local temple. A superstition says that if a Chinese person stops by a local temple and talks about all the good and bad they have encountered that past year, it will bring them good luck and good fortune for the upcoming year. Some lucky Chinese workers will even receive a bonus as a token of thanks and good fortune in the upcoming year.

Chinese Tourism

People are fascinated with China's long, ancient history, gorgeous modern cities, culture, and the country's natural wonders and eagerly want to visit the country. In fact, China is the third busiest tourist destination after France and the United States. An estimated 98.8 million tourists travel to the nation each year. While many tourists are from other Asian countries, such as South Korea, Japan, Vietnam, Malaysia, and Mongolia, tourists from the United States and Canada also arrive in China. The most popular destinations for tourists are Beijing, Hong Kong, Shenzhen, Shanghai, and Xi'an, and the Great Wall of China.

Tianjin

Tianjin is one of the four main urban areas in China. Its name derives from the Chinese for "the place where the emperor crossed the river." Tianjin's coastal position means that it is ideally located as a transport hub and also as a center for international business. For centuries, Tianjin has attracted travelers from across China and the rest of the world. As a result of this, the city has evolved into a vibrant and interesting cosmopolitan area full of different ethnicities and cultures.

The bustling city of Tianjin today, is home to one of the largest artificially constructed harbors in northern China. Ships depart from the harbor for important

Tianjin eye is the most popular modern landmark in the city.

A historical street in Tianjin with traditional Chinese architecture.

destinations throughout the world. In recent years, Tianjin has become a hub for cruise liners to dock, and hence Tianjin is now an important tourist destination, too.

Throughout history, Tianjin has seen political influence from foreign powers as well as commercial. From 1860 to 1903, the United Kingdom, the USA, France, Germany, Japan, Russia, Italy, Belgium, and other western nations forced the Qing régime to cede eastern Tianjin to them, dividing it up among themselves. These foreign powers constructed their buildings in their own traditional styles, leading to a jumble of different architectural styles in a relatively small area. Standing in contrast to the older buildings are the city's many modern skyscrapers, including the iconic Tianjin Radio and Television Tower, an impressive sight for all travelers to see.

European influences can clearly be seen on this bridge crossing the Haihe River in the center of Tianjin.

RESEARCH PROJECT

The Great Wall of China has been through many battles, both during the building process and after it was completed. Create a brief presentation about one of these battles that took place and almost destroyed the wall.

TEXT-DEPENDENT QUESTIONS

1. What was the name of China's capital before it became Beijing?

2. What city was awarded best attractive city for the fourth time in 2016?

3. What islands are accessible only by ferry in Hong Kong?

The financial center of Shanghai is home to many impressive buildings.

WORDS TO UNDERSTAND

famine: a drastic long-term, wide-reaching food shortage that results in many deaths

pollutant: a substance introduced into the environment that has undesired effects, causing long- or short-term damage

regulation: a law, rule, or other order prescribed by authority, especially to regulate conduct

reservoir: a natural or artificial pond or lake used for the storage and regulation of water

A BRIGHT FUTURE FOR CHINA

Despite the many problems faced by China in 2019—a large population, pollution, economic instability, food scares, unbalanced social services, and more—there is still a bright future ahead for China with a new generation taking over the country. But how will this new generation of leaders govern this powerful and complex nation? China is an economic success story with people who have suffered from wars and under dynasties and Communist rule, but through all this, China has proven to be unstoppable.

Development

China's future depends on further development in the economic sector. During the beginning of the 2010s, 30 million new homes were built, along with miles of new railroad tracks and reinforced **reservoirs**. The central aim of the government is to continue to grow economically. This means that pensions need to be secured, issues of corruption dealt with, and measures taken to deal with the strangling pollution that affects the air and soil of this massive nation.

China is a densely populated country. This aerial view illustrates how closely houses are packed together in China.

New Regulations

Since the 2010s, the Communist Party in China is losing its authority over the nation. Hopefully, new leaders will introduce new measures to combat the problems that arose during China's rapid economic growth when the Communist regime took over.

When it comes to clearing the choking pollution, China needs to impose regulations on air **pollutants** and how waste is disposed of. However, this will drive up costs on industries that are responsible for the country's economic growth. Some industries are owned by the Communist state, while others are privately owned. This produces fierce competition among the private companies, who seem unable—or unwilling—to clean up their act. The cost of correcting over 100 years of unregulated pollution may be too much for some industries to bear. New **regulations** could force companies to cut back on the number of workers they hire, so China's leaders will have to weigh the cost of reducing pollution against dealing with higher unemployment rates.

China's new leader, Xi Jinping, will have to make many decisions about imposing regulations throughout the country. According to the new leader, China plans to open its economy but doesn't have any plans to change its political system. This means China will continue to build giant cities and smaller towns in trying to shift its population away from country dwelling and into urban dwelling.

China and the Rest of the World

Will China continue to be a stabilizing force for peace, security, and global economics into the future? This depends on a number of factors. For example, China and U.S. relations have weakened as the United States points out China's human rights abuses. Also, the current U.S. administration is making changes with regards to terms of trade with China. Another factor is that China continues to build missiles, which undermines peace and stability in the world. The United States is also concerned about China's neighbor, North Korea, and the instability this nation brings to the world.

While the United States can help lead China in the right direction, it cannot force the huge country to create any new laws or political and economic reforms. However, it is important for the United States to continue to work with China on issues, just as the rest of the world's countries continue to work together. Negotiating trade terms, developing a rule of law, and creating an economic partnership are projects that will benefit both nations and the world at large.

What is Communism?

Communism was first introduced by Karl Marx in 1848. At its core, communism removes from citizens the right to personal possessions, including homes and businesses. It also removes social classes, property rights, and inheritance rights. Communist governments, like the one in China, control all of a society's transportation, communication, education, and agriculture. The goal of communism is to divide natural resources equally among its population. It goes on further to

A statue of China's former leader Mao Zedong in the city of Kashgar.

control human resources, such as talent and creativity. All in all, a Communist government controls nearly everything in the society it rules over.

Communism and Agriculture in China

There is no question that communism has affected agriculture in China. The first Communist leader, Mao Zedong, implemented an investment strategy to help develop and distribute food that was produced equally across the nation. At first this worked, with plenty of crops producing enough food to feed the country. However, Mao decided to take it a step further by initiating the "Great Leap Forward," which took privately owned farms and turned them into common areas where everyone worked the land. Unfortunately, this didn't work out because the people were unable to adapt to the new system, and then the country had to deal with poor soil and bad weather. This led to a severe **famine** in China that killed 30 million people.

Communism and the Economy of China

While communism's goal is to put the power in the people's hands, in China the process was overseen by an elite few of government officials. The point was to gather all resources and evenly distribute them among the nation's citizens but the government, fueled by corruption, often took more than its fair share.

At the start of communism in China, the country experienced economic increase. But during the first five years of the "Great Leap Forward," peasants were expected to forge their own tools, which took them away from the fields. Since the farmers weren't experts at tool forging, the tools they produced were of poor quality. Having individual farmers make their own tools also used a tremendous amount of coal that was needed to run the railway system.

Tiananmen Square is the location of the famous pro-democracy protests in 1989. Thousands of people were either killed or injured.

After a seven year slump, the Chinese economy is improving which is good news for its citizens, young and old.

Communism and Culture

The Cultural Revolution imposed by Mao meant to destroy everything of China's old culture—as well as all outside influences—to create a new China. His philosophy demanded complete loyalty to the state over loyalty to the family. This caused many people to turn against their own family members and went directly against the Confucius philosophy that children should respect their parents and other family members.

In the end, the policy was a disaster for the culture of China as the Red Guard was created, schools were closed, books about ancient China were destroyed, and the family unit began to break down. All in all, communism has shaped modern Chinese culture, including agriculture and the economy.

China's Economy Today

According to the Chinese government, the economy is growing again after a seven year slump. This means the government now has the ability to improve social service, education, and pollution issues. Whether they will or not is anybody's guess. With such a large nation as China, it can be difficult to analyze the country's current economic health. In fact, outside experts challenge the assumption that China's economy has grown and instead imply that it has weakened.

China has seen growth in exports and the property market has grown, meaning China might be in a better position to tackle debt—another problem affecting the economy. However, this growth comes at a price. China has had to borrow money to stay in the game and has yet to tackle important problems like pollution and social issues. These social problems come in the form of parents leaving children behind in rural areas to find work in urban areas, which further breaks down the family unit. Overall,

Mao Zedong

Mao Zedong was born on December 26, 1893 in Shaoshan, China, and died on September 9, 1976, in Beijing. He was a Marxist theorist and soldier who led the country into communism following the Cultural Revolution. To modern historians, he is considered the dominant force that moved China into a new era.

Having been the son of a peasant, Mao was all too familiar with the hardships of peasant life and sought to change this. However, his father was successful and encouraged Mao's education. He attended school until he was thirteen and then worked on his father's farm. At this time, he began to rebel against old traditions, including arranged marriages, and left his family farm to pursue his education in Changsha.

After trying to pursue careers in law and business, he eventually joined the Communist Party and in 1920 he married Yang Kaihui, who stood beside him as he brought the country under Communist rule in 1949. From here, he led China down a road of modernization and economic stability by rejecting the old ways of his country, as well as all Western influence.

China is finally taking the use of renewable energy seriously. This solar plant is supplying energy to Shanghai.

China seems to be putting more emphasis on economic growth over fixing the problems created from the rise of the Communist Party in China.

Renewable Energy in China

China seeks to become a green superpower in the future. In fact, the nation invests more money into renewable energy than any other country. Annually, it budgets about $126 million USD for the industry and that amount is expected to increase each year. China is especially interested in solar power and aims to generate enough power from the sun to supply more than 30 million homes with electricity.

This initiative is part of a plan to cut back on carbon emissions and improve the country's pollution problem. By 2030, China hopes to decrease its dependence on fossil fuels, including coal, by 20 percent. The burning of coal for energy is directly related to pollution-caused deaths in China. In fact, it is estimated that many thousands of Chinese citizens die prematurely from pollution each year.

China Today and in the Future

China has had tremendous effects on its neighbors. Most of the East Asia region has been influenced by Chinese culture, including Japan, Korea, and even in Southeast Asia, including Vietnam, where many Chinese immigrated to in the past. Buddhism may not be thriving in China, but it spread to India and Tibet where it is practiced by a large majority of these populations. China also does business in Indonesia, Singapore, Malaysia, Cambodia, and Thailand, forming a solid relationship with these countries. Even the small nation of Eritrea on the Horn of Africa trades with China, so it definitely has a far reach in the world's economy.

At one point, China remained completely isolated from the world for thirty years. During this time, the Chinese Communist Party sought to support other Communist parties in other countries where many Chinese people lived. However, the locals of these countries often looked upon these groups with suspicion and hostility.

However, when Deng came to power in 1978, he began changing this situation. First he removed support for Communists living outside of China and demanded that they show loyalty to the countries where the immigrants were living, rather than to China. This helped forge trusting relationships between China and its neighbors. One reason Deng did this was to encourage the Chinese people living in other countries to invest in their motherland. This helped spur China's economic growth.

From the 1970s to the 2010s, China has really focused on creating a relationship with the United States and the Soviet Union, which collapsed in 1991. The Chinese government viewed a good relationship with the United States as a primary route to enter the international community and modernize their country. Unfortunately, after the Tiananmen Square Massacre in 1989, the United States and other Western nations, including Canada, imposed sanctions on China for human rights abuses. This led China to forge relationships with other Asian countries who had no interest in imposing their views upon China like the West did. China created connections with Taiwan, Japan, and South Korea and found itself breaking open the isolation imposed by the West with these new relationships in Asia. Many people saw an opportunity in China and took it, helping to transform China's struggling political and economic systems.

China enjoys trading with the United States in 2019, its biggest trade partner, and with Canada. In the year 2000, President Bill Clinton signed the U.S.-China Relations Act that allowed for trade relations with the United States, paving the way for China to join the World Trade Organization in 2001. Nearing the year 2020, China is the biggest trade partner with the United States in the world.

China's Future Remains Uncertain

As trading continues with the United States and other nations, China is currently considered a superpower on the economic world stage. Recently, the Chinese government did away with a controversial one-child policy and now allows citizens to have two children. The one-child policy was implemented in an effort to control overpopulation. However, many people still had more than one child and did not register the child's birth, making them unable to benefit from being a Chinese citizen. Many of these children simply do not exist, according to the government, and therefore cannot attend school.

So the state control over Chinese citizens' day-to-day lives is still apparent in 2019. However, with new leadership and efforts to improve both the economy and the pollution problem, China strives to gain a better future for its country and its citizens.

RESEARCH PROJECT

Create a brief presentation on how communism has affected China's economy.

TEXT-DEPENDENT QUESTIONS

1. What renewable energies does China use?

2. What are three problems facing China's economy in the 2010s?

3. Why did China introduce a one-child policy?

CHINESE FOOD

"Chinese food" is famous and is found all over the world. However, the Chinese have their own eating customs and dishes that are unique to the country. For example, the Chinese will never eat food that has dropped on the table. There is no five-second rule in China! They share food communally and tend to eat sweets before or during the meal. They also eat rice or noodles every day and drink hot water with their meal to aid in digestion.

Here are two popular Chinese dishes, along with the instructions on how to make them.

Hunan Chicken
Makes 4 servings

Ingredients
3 tablespoons canola oil, divided
4 boneless, skinless chicken thighs, cut
1-inch pieces
1-inch piece ginger, minced
1 large head broccoli, cut into small
 florets
10 medium sided mushrooms, sliced
4–6 whole dried chilies
2 tablespoons sherry
¼ cup low-sodium soy sauce
1 teaspoon cornstarch
2 teaspoons sambal oelek
1 teaspoon sesame oil
Rice, for serving

Directions
1. Heat 2 tablespoons of canola oil in a large skillet over medium heat. Add the chicken and cook until done.

2. Add the leftover oil in the same pan along with ginger.

3. Then add the broccoli, mushrooms, and red chilies.

4. Cook until done, about 5 minutes. Serve on a bed of rice with the sauce.

5. To make the sauce, combine sherry, cornstarch, soy sauce, sesame oil, and sambal oelek in a small pan and simmer until the sauce thickens.

Pan-Seared Sichuan Shrimp with Noodles

Makes 4 servings

Ingredients

6 ounces dried noodles
1 pound medium shrimp, shelled and
 deveined
Salt and freshly ground white pepper
1 red chili, sliced
1 teaspoon ground Sichuan peppercorns
3 tablespoons vegetable oil
4 large scallions, thinly sliced
2 tablespoons finely grated fresh ginger
⅓ cup soy sauce or tamari
3 tablespoons Chinese black vinegar or
 balsamic vinegar
1½ teaspoons chili oil

Directions

1. To start, bring a large saucepan of water to a boil.

2. In the meantime, cover noodles in a bowl with warm water and let stand about 5 minutes.

3. Next, drain the noodles and cut them into lengths of 4 inches. Place the noodles in the saucepan and let them boil for about 25 seconds. Drain and return them to the pan.

4. Season the shrimp with salt and pepper and fry them in a large skillet with vegetable oil. Add the remaining ingredients and simmer until done.

FESTIVALS & HOLIDAYS

Each year, China holds several legal holidays. These include New Year's Day, Chinese New Year (also known as the Spring Festival), Qingming Festival, May Day, the Dragon Boat Festival, Mid-Autumn Day, and National Day.

Chinese New Year is the biggest and most important festival. It takes place over a seven day period and is a colorful event dominated by red lanterns, fireworks, parades, and banquets. Preparation for this big holiday starts with the Chinese cleaning their houses. They believe this is a way to put the past year behind them as they usher in the New Year with hopes of good fortune.

The Dragon Boat Festival has been observed for over 2,000 years. The purpose of this festival is to commemorate the Chinese poet Qu Yuan. The holiday lasts three days starting on the fifth day of the fifth month of a new year, according to the lunar calendar. Celebrations include dragon boat racing and eating sticky rice dumplings, among other ways to celebrate this holiday. Overall, the holiday is filled with tradition and superstition, most likely originating from dragon worship in ancient times. The celebration is so old that UNESCO (the United Nations Educational, Scientific and Cultural Organization) added it to the World Intangible Cultural Heritage list.

The Qingming Festival, also known as the Festival of Pure Brightness, takes place each year on April 4th or 5th, according to the Gregorian calendar. Because it takes place in the spring, it holds a special connection to agriculture. Temperatures rise and rain begins to

86   CHINA

fall in the spring, hopefully producing healthy crops. The festival is also a day to commemorate the dead. The Chinese have a history of ancestor worship, which makes this festival especially important.

During the festival, people also fly kites during the day and evening. They tie small lanterns to the end of the kites and when the kites fly in the sky, the lanterns look like small, twinkling stars. Then the string is cut and the kite, along with the lantern, is set free. This is said to bring good luck.

National Day in China was founded in 1949 and celebrates the creation of the Central People's Government with government-sponsored fireworks and concerts. It is observed every year on October 1 because this was the day the People's Republic of China was founded. In the 1950s, the day was celebrated with massive military parades.

Series Glossary
of Key Terms

aboriginal	Of or relating to the original people living in a region.
archaeology	A science that deals with past human life and activities as shown by objects (as pottery, tools, and statues) left by ancient peoples.
archipelago	A group of islands.
biomass	A renewable energy source from living or recently living plant and animal materials, which can be used as fuel.
Borneo	An island of the Malay Archipelago southwest of the Philippines and divided between Brunei, Malaysia, and Indonesia.
boundary	Something that indicates or fixes a limit or extent.
Buddhism	A religion of eastern and central Asia based on the teachings of Gautama Buddha.
Christianity	A religion based on the teachings of Jesus Christ.
civilization	An advanced stage (as in art, science, and government) in the development of society.
colony	A distant territory belonging to or under the control of a nation.
commodity	Something produced by agriculture, mining, or manufacture.
Confucianism	Of or relating to the Chinese philosopher Confucius or his teachings or followers.
culture	The habits, beliefs, and traditions of a particular people, place, or time.
dialect	A form of a language that is spoken in a certain region or by a certain group.
diversity	The condition or fact of being different.
economic boom	A period of increased commercial activity within either a business, market, industry, or economy as a whole.
emerging market	An emerging market economy is a nation's economy that is progressing toward becoming advanced.
endangered species	A species threatened with extinction.
enterprise	A business organization or activity.
European Union	An economic, scientific, and political organization consisting of 27 European countries.
foreign exchange reserve	Foreign currency reserves that are held by the central bank of a country.
geothermal energy	Energy stored in the form of heat beneath the earth's surface. It is a carbon-free, renewable, and sustainable form of energy.
global warming	A warming of the earth's atmosphere and oceans that is thought to be a result of air pollution.

Hindu	A person who follows Hinduism.
independence	The quality or state of not being under the control of, reliant on, or connected with someone or something else.
industrialization	The widespread development of industries in a region, country, or culture.
infrastructure	The system of public works of a country, state, or region.
interest rate	The proportion of a loan that is charged as interest to the borrower, typically expressed as an annual percentage of the loan outstanding.
Islam	The religious faith of Muslims including belief in Allah as the sole deity and in Muhammad as his prophet.
land reclamation	The process of creating new land from oceans, riverbeds, or lake beds.
landmass	A large area of land.
Malay	A member of a people of the Malay Peninsula, eastern Sumatra, parts of Borneo, and some adjacent islands.
Mandarin	The chief dialect of China.
maritime	Of or relating to ocean navigation or trade.
Mongol	A member of any of a group of traditionally pastoral peoples of Mongolia.
monsoon	The rainy season that occurs in southern Asia in the summer.
mortality rate	The number of a particular group who die each year.
natural resource	Something (as water, a mineral, forest, or kind of animal) that is found in nature and is valuable to humans.
peninsula	A piece of land extending out into a body of water.
precipitation	Water that falls to the earth as hail, mist, rain, sleet, or snow.
recession	A period of reduced business activity.
republic	A country with elected representatives and an elected chief of state who is not a monarch and who is usually a president.
Ring of Fire	Belt of volcanoes and frequent seismic activity nearly encircling the Pacific Ocean.
Shintoism	The indigenous religion of Japan.
street food	Prepared or cooked food sold by vendors in a street or other public location for immediate consumption.
sultan	A ruler especially of a Muslim state.
Taoism	A religion developed from Taoist philosophy and folk and Buddhist religion and concerned with obtaining long life and good fortune often by magical means.
tiger economy	A tiger economy is a nickname given to several booming economies in Southeast Asia.
typhoon	A hurricane occurring especially in the region of the Philippines or the China Sea.
urbanization	The process by which towns and cities are formed and become larger as more and more people begin living and working in central areas.

Chronology

ca. 1700-1046 BCE: Shang Dynasty.

1045-ca. 770 Zhou Dynasty.

ca. 770 Zhou state collapses.

221–206 King Ying Zheng of Qin unites much of the Chinese heartland.

206 BCE–220 CE: Han Dynasty.

220-589: Collapse of Han state.

618-907: Tang Dynasty.

960-1279: Song Dynasty.

1271-1368: Mongols conquer China and establish the Yuan Dynasty.

1368: Ming Dynasty overthrows Mongols.

1644: Manchu Qing Dynasty drives out Ming.

19th c.: Qing Dynasty begins a long decline.

1899–1901: "Boxer Rebellion" in Northern China.

1911–12: Military revolts lead to proclamation of Republic of China.

1931–45: Japan invades and gradually occupies China.

1934-35: Mao Zedong emerges as Communist leader.

1949: Mao Zedong proclaims the founding of the People's Republic of China.

1966–76: "Cultural Revolution."

1992: The International Monetary Fund (IMF) ranks China's economy as third largest in the world after the U.S. and Japan.

2009: China stages mass celebrations to mark 60 years since the Communist Party came to power.

2017: The country's economic growth slows, with 2016 marking its slowest growth since 1990.

2018: China announces it will impose 25 percent trade tariffs on various U.S. goods, including soybeans, cars, and orange juice, in retaliation for similar U.S. tariffs on about 1,300 Chinese products.

Further Reading

Dikotter, Frank. *The Cultural Revolution: A People's History 1962–1976.* London: Bloomsbury Press, 2016.

Fenby, Jonathan. *Will China Dominate the 21st Century?* Cambridge: Polity Press, 2017.

Kroeber, Arthur R. *China's Economy: What Everyone Needs to Know.* New York: Oxford University Press, 2016.

Liu, Jing. *The Making of Modern China: The Ming Dynasty to the Qing Dynasty (1368–1912).* Stone Bridge Press, 2017.

Internet Resources

http://www.pbs.org/story-china/home
PBS is a nonprofit educational portal that covers many topics, including the history of China.

https://www.weforum.org/agenda/2016/06/8-facts-about-chinas-economy
The World Economic Forum gives vital information about China's economy.

https://www.chinahighlights.com/travelguide/most-famous-cities.htm
This site highlights the different popular cities of China.

https://www.chinahighlights.com/beijing/forbidden-city
Learn fun facts about the Forbidden City!

The websites listed on this page were active at the time of publication. The publisher is not responsible for websites that have changed their addresses or discontinued operation since the date of publication. The publisher will review and update the website list upon each reprint.

Index

Organizations to Contact

For general inquiries into traveling in China and for brochure requests, contact:

STA Travel

722 Broadway, New York NY 10003

Phone: (212) 473-6100, Toll Free: 800-781-4040

Website: www.statravel.com

U.S. Embassy Beijing

55 Anjialou Rd., Chaoyang District, Beijing, China, 100600

Website: https://china.usembassy-china.org.cn

China National Tourist Office

New York, 270 Lexington Ave., Suite 912, New York 10017

Phone: (212) 760-8218 E-mail: www.cnto.org

Website: www.cnto.org

U.S. Chinese Culture Center

1708 Greene St., Columbia, SC 29201

Phone: (803) 252-9086

E-mail usccc@chineseculturecenter.org

Website: webmaster@chineseculturecenter.org

Author's Biography

Jennifer Brown has a BA in English from the University of Rhode Island and a BA in education from the University of Windsor. She has traveled the world as an educator, living and working in countries such as Ethiopia, Eritrea, and Mexico. Jennifer lives with her family in Seattle, Washington, where she works as a writer and runs a nonprofit called the Brown Mission Society, whose aim is to reduce poverty and improve education and health care in the developing world. When not working, Jennifer enjoys traveling, spending time with her family, and reading. Originally from Rhode Island, Jennifer has enjoyed living in many countries and cities around the world.

Picture Credits

Video Credits

Page 14: MrZoller, http://x-qr.net/1Ks6
Page 22: laowhy86, http://x-qr.net/1J6p
Page 41: BBC News, http://x-qr.net/1LEy
Page 47: CGTN America, http://x-qr.net/1Hvt
Page 56: Plethrons, http://x-qr.net/1KJc